B r e a

Stress

a w a y

DAVID BROOKES

Copyright 1997 David Brookes

ISBN 0 9527105 52

Hollanden Publishing Ltd
Chancery Lane
Beckenham
Kent
BR3 6NR

Printed and bound in
The United Kingdom
by Mattrix Printers, Tonbridge,
Kent

First Impression

The author of *Breathe Stress Away* does not dispense medical advice nor prescribe the use of any technique as a form of treatment for physical or medical problems without the advice of a physician either directly or indirectly. In the interests of good health, it is always important to consult your doctor before commencing any diet or exercise programme. The intent of the author is only to offer information of a general nature to help you in the quest for your holistic well being. In the event that you use any of the information in this book for yourself, the author and publisher assume no responsibility for your actions.

ACKNOWLEDGMENTS

My thanks to Peter Phillips, who has the remarkable ability to catch the spark of an idea and fan the flames with an energy, focus and enthusiasm that makes books happen.

A special thank you to Dr. Ashley Conway for his substantial contribution to the chapter on hyperventilation, and whose profound knowledge and advice has been vital in the development of the book. Thanks also to Siv Brookes for her contribution to Breathing and The Alexander Technique.

My sincere thanks to Cangy, Rachael and Karen for their invaluable contributions.

Edited by Cangy Venables

Designed by Rachael Parfitt

Illustrations by Karen Cochrane

"Universal peace starts within each individual.
It is like a stone thrown into a pool of water.
The ripples go out and out but they start at
the very centre. When we find that peace
and harmony within us, then the ripples from
the centre of peace within us will reverberate
and go out to the world........."

FINDHORN

FOREWORD

Breathing is essential to support life, and we all do it automatically. So why should be need a book explaining how to breathe correctly? There are a number of important reasons.

The stresses of modern life may have a profound influence on the way the we breathe – causing over-breathing, breath holding, and a change in the style and rhythm of our breathing. To restore a healthy, natural breathing pattern may require a conscious effort on our part.

The way in which we breathe influences the way we think and feel. There is a vicious circle between psychological stress and disordered breathing – each has an effect on the other. Of all the bodily functions necessary to support life, breathing is the one most open to conscious control. It would be difficult to consciously change our heart rate or gut movement, but we **can** change our breathing.

The way that we breathe can affect the heart, the nerves, blood flow, kidney functioning, electrical activity in the brain and many other systems. While it would be difficult to influence these systems directly, they can benefit indirectly from healthy breathing.

In this concise book, David Brookes provides valuable information about breathing and details beneficial exercises that can help to calm or stimulate, according to the need. Read it thoughtfully, do the exercises with patience and enjoy the benefits.

Dr. Ashley Conway

INTRODUCTION

We cannot exist without breathing – if the body is deprived of oxygen we die within minutes. A healthy intake of oxygen is vital to both our physical and mental well-being. For thousands of years many ancient traditions, including Yoga, Chi king and T'ai chi have used breath control as one of the most basic forms of meditation.

Yogis have developed it into a science, with the aim of utilizing the air we breathe by teaching mind and body to function as one. Yet many of us regard breathing with indifference, as a mere functional activity, without considering **how** we breathe.

Breathing should be slow and rhythmical; above all, breathing should be relaxed. However, the high-tech, high-speed world that we inhabit is not conducive to healthy breathing: family problems, pressures at work and financial worries can all create prolonged stress.

Unhealthy stress can severely damage both our minds and bodies, breathing problems being a classic symptom. When we are tense our breathing becomes shallow and rigid; yet many of us are unaware that we are breathing incorrectly, thereby exacerbating the tensions and frustrations already present.

Susbsequently, many people have lost the art of healthy breathing. Through simple breathing and relaxation exercises, it is possible to rectify the problem. And, as you learn to breathe correctly, you can simultaneously establish a relaxed state of mind.

Many physical problems can also be relieved.

The most important thing to
bear in mind as you go
through this book is that
breathing is a natural process.
Some of the exercises included
have a specific purpose, but
overall the aim should be to
correct any incorrect breathing
so that it once again becomes
relaxed, natural and balanced.
With this will come a renewed
sense of health and vitality –
themselves a great tool to
combat the dangers of stress.

CONTENTS

WHAT IS STRESS?

WHAT IS STRESS?

The debilitating effects of stress, caused by constant pressure both at work and home, are a modern phenomenon. However, stress or at least temporary stress, is a very necessary part of our lives. One important function of short-term stress is to channel our resources to deal with challenging or even life-threatening situations.

Temporary stress, therefore, allows us an extra turn of speed in escaping danger; it increases the speed of our reactions when, for example, avoiding a collision while driving; it recharges a mentally or physically exhausted body to cope with greater challenges, and boosts an athlete's performance during an important event.

In prehistoric times, this bodily reaction to stress was exactly what was needed. This is attributed to physiological changes that occurred to the body when danger appeared. Chemicals, especially adrenalin, were released into the body and prepared it for fight or flight. The heart beat faster, blood supply was transferred from the non-essential to the essential; from the skin and digestive organs to the muscles and the head.

This resulted both in clearer, swifter thinking and faster, stronger muscular responses. The lungs took in more oxygen, breathing became more rapid, and the body anticipated keeping cool by increasing perspiration. Once the danger had passed or fighting or fleeing had occurred (successfully!), the bodily functions reverted to normal.

In prehistoric times, these bodily responses were vital for survival, and the internal energy responses were used

Today, however, the problems and stresses that we experience have changed radically and can rarely be resolved with physical action. We are not designed to operate effectively in this hi-tech world. Hunting for food is now replaced by jostling with our trolleys in supermarkets!

Psychological stresses lead to the same bodily state of arousal as does fight and flight, but mostly without any accompanying physical activity to use up the adrenalin and energy made available. When this stress is prolonged, physical and mental damage will occur, sometimes resulting in serious disease.

OUR PHYSICAL RESPONSES TO STRESS INCLUDE:

- HUNCHING OUR SHOULDERS
- CLENCHING OUR TEETH
- FROWNING
- TIGHTENING OUR NECKS
- STOOPING

LONG PERIODS OF STRESS CAN LEAD TO:

- LOSS OF APPETITE
- LACK OF ENERGY
- BREATHLESSNESS
- FREQUENT SWEATING
- TIGHTENING IN THE CHEST
- PAIN IN THE NECK OR SHOULDERS
- LACK OF CONCENTRATION
- INDECISIVENESS
- ANXIETY
- INSOMNIA

MORE SEVERE SYMPTOMS MAY FOLLOW, SUCH AS:

- SKIN RASHES
- ALLERGIES
- ACUTE ANXIETY
- DEPRESSION
- MIGRAINE
- DIGESTIVE DISORDERS, INCLUDING ULCERS AND COLITIS
- IRRITABLE BOWEL SYNDROME
- HIGH BLOOD PRESSURE

11

PLEASE NOTE:

Do not assume that your symptoms are solely related to stress. Always seek medical advice before taking any action.

STRESS AND BREATHING

HOW ARE THEY RELATED?

"To breathe healthily is a gift from nature. To work against nature is to work against life"

YOGIC PROVERB

STRESS AND BREATHING

HOW ARE THEY RELATED?

A functional necessity that most of us take for granted, breathing can be seriously affected by stress. As our breathing becomes rigid and shallow, so our tensions will accumulate. Your mind tells you to breathe more deeply but your body tension prevents it. As our tensions accumulate, so our breathing becomes more jerky and increasingly ineffective.

When stressed, some of us pause in our breathing when needing to think; others might breathe shallowly, using only a fraction of the lungs' capacity. Some of us even gulp breaths.

When tense or stressed, a brisk walk can be enormously beneficial. By setting a rhythmic pace, the breathing also becomes rhythmic and the act of simple, not too energetic, exercise activates the dormant portion of our lungs. After only a relatively short walk, tension disappears and by breathing rhythmically and fully, we feel mentally and physically refreshed.

Breathing is the one vital function over which we can have control. Deep, steady breathing can be an indispensable tool in stressful situations.

No one teaches babies how to breathe. Breathing is an automatic response and, just as our posture can deterioriate as we grow older, so too our breathing techniques can deteriorate with physiological changes as a result of progressive stress.

Just as stress affects our breathing, so too can our breathing affect stress. Rhythmic full breathing encourages us to relax and

15

arouses what is termed the parasympathetic response, which counters or switches off the fight and flight response.

In effect, healthy, relaxed breathing is a way of approaching and solving a problem "top down", as opposed to "bottom up". For example, when angry or sad, your facial expressions exhibit your inner feelings. At times like this the very idea of smiling might be a total anathema. You have to wait until your mood reverts to a more happy state.

However, if during these depressive or angry moods you actually force a smile, this very act of smiling can release endorphines into the body. These endorphines can result in a total mood change to one of happiness.

It is important to recognise that correct, relaxed deep breathing cannot co-exist with stress and that the harmful sequence of:

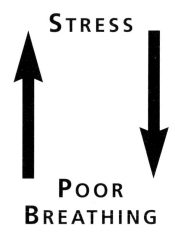

STRESS

POOR BREATHING

NEEDS TO BE BROKEN

THE FIRST STEPS

Changing habits of a lifetime is not easy. The desire to take responsibility for yourself is vital; you must also be prepared to practice regularly.

Most manifestions of relaxation depend on controlled breathing; breathing and relaxation are inseparable.

As you practice correct healthy breathing, it will eventually become habit and part of your physical and mental makeup.

PHYSICAL BENEFITS OF HEALTHY BREATHING

- RAPIDLY REDUCES STRESS LEVELS
- MAXIMIZES OXYGEN INTAKE
- VITALIZES THE BODY

17

HYPERVENTILATION

"Breath is the bridge which connects life to consciousness which unites your body to your thoughts. Whenever your mind becomes scattered, use your breath as the means to take hold of your mind again"

THICH NHAT HANH

HYPERVENTILATION

As explained in the previous chapter, breathing and stress are closely linked. Unhealthy breathing – and hyperventilation – can be both the cause and result of stress symptoms.

Commonly known as over-breathing, hyperventilation is properly defined as "Breathing in excess of metabolic requirements", which means breathing more than you need to. When this happens, the proportion of carbon dioxide dissolved in the blood is reduced – which affects its balance of acidity and alkalinity. Blood goes all around the body so all the body cells are affected.

WHY DO PEOPLE HYPERVENTILATE?

There are many different factors which can trigger hyperventilation. These can broadly be divided in physical and psychological.

PHYSICAL TRIGGERS INCLUDE:

- PAIN
- EXHAUSTION
- HANGOVER
- DRUG WITHDRAWAL (INCLUDING ALCOHOL AND TRANQUILIZERS)
- HORMONAL CHANGES DURING THE MENSTRUAL CYCLE
- FEVER

PSYCHOLOGICAL TRIGGERS INCLUDE:

- STRESS – THE FIGHT OR FLIGHT RESPONSE
- ANXIETY
- STRONG EMOTIONAL AROUSAL, ESPECIALLY IF WHEN OVER A LONG PERIOD OF TIME OR UNEXPRESSED

There may be an obvious major emotional trauma preceding the onset of hyperventilation or sometimes there is a gradual build-up – it is often attributed to a number of factors.

SYMPTOMS

Hyperventilation can produce a wide range of symptoms, which can often be frightening to the individual and can sometimes make accurate diagnosis difficult.

PHYSICAL SYMPTOMS INCLUDE:

- DIZZINESS
- LIGHT-HEADEDNESS
- TINGLING OR NUMBNESS
- MUSCLE TENSION
- VISUAL DISTURBANCES
- HEADACHES
- PALPITATIONS
- BREATHLESSNESS
- EXHAUSTION
- CHANGE IN BREATHING PATTERN CAN ALSO CAUSE CHEST PAIN

PSYCHOLOGICAL SYMPTOMS INCLUDE:

- ANXIETY
- PANIC
- OCCASIONAL FEELINGS OF UNREALITY
- FEAR OF FAINTING
- DEPRESSION
- FEAR THAT SOMETHING IS SERIOUSLY WRONG PHYSICALLY

Hyperventilation can be **chronic** – going on most of the time. Or it can be **acute** – breathing may be normal most of the time, but suddenly switch into hyperventilation.

WHAT HAPPENS DURING HYPERVENTILATION?

There are a number of important physical changes that hyperventilation induces in the body:

1. NERVE CELLS. At first these may become very sensitive, firing more easily, and subsequently become exhausted.

2. HEART RATE GOES UP. Some people are more aware of this than others – the heart rate may feel as though it is irregular.

3. OXYGEN DISASSOCIATION TAKES PLACE. As the blood becomes more alkaline as a result of hyperventilation, the red blood cells release oxygen less easily. This can have the paradoxical effect that despite the fact that hyperventilation involves over-breathing, the cells of the body may actually have less oxygen available to them.

4. VASOCONSTRICTION. Blood vessels narrow down in response to hyperventilation.

How can hyperventilation be helped?

By the time hyperventilation is identified, a vicious circle has often been established.

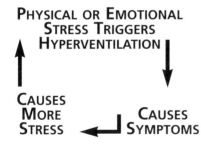

PHYSICAL OR EMOTIONAL STRESS TRIGGERS HYPERVENTILATION

CAUSES MORE STRESS ← **CAUSES SYMPTOMS**

As the fear intensity of this viscious circle continues or escalates, it might develop into a panic attack which is an additional problem associated with faulty breathing. Therefore, there may be a number of different levels at which it is appropriate to intervene to break up this cycle, all of which may be important.

1. Understand what is going on.

2. Deal with the factors causing the hyperventilation. These may be physical; for example, sleep disturbances, over-use of stimulants such as caffeine, or long-term exhaustion. The cause may be emotional – finding ways to deal with bottled up emotions is often very helpful.

3. Manipulate the breathing. There are three possible ways to restore the carbon dioxide balance and relieve the symptoms:

SHORT TERM MEASURES

1. Put carbon dioxide into the system by breathing for a few minutes **only** into a paper bag held over the mouth. The same (but a more discreet) effect can be created by rebreathing into cupped hands.

2. Increase the rate of carbon dioxide production – using major muscle groups may help; exercise such as pacing up and down is an example.

LONG TERM MEASURES

Reduce the amount of air that you are breathing. This will restore the acid balance of the blood, calm the nervous system, slow the heart rate, cause blood vessels to dilate and allow oxygen that is present in the blood to be released more easily to the body.

Breathing slowly is good for the body; if you have a healthy pair of lungs it is virtually impossible to underbreathe. Breathe through your nose, slowly, and low down in your tummy. Your chest should barely move. Breathing should be slow and regular – avoid breath holding and sighing. When you talk, speak reasonably slowly. This type of breathing will not only encourage a calmer disposition, it will also help you keep that way.

Only you can achieve this – it will demand some practice to retrain your body to breathe efficiently – but the benefits will make the effort well worthwhile.

If you have any of the above symptoms, you should consult your doctor to establish the cause and the appropriate treatment, as the symptoms may not be attributable to hyperventilation. Do not attempt the deep-breathing techniques mentioned in other parts of the book if you are hyperventilating.

THE THEORY OF HEALTHY BREATHING

"To master our breath is to be in conrol of
our bodies and minds"

THICH MHAT HANH

THE PHYSIOLOGY OF BREATHING

Our lungs usually inhale and exhale around 500 cubic centimetres of air, but when forcing a full breath, we can breathe in six times as much.

Similarly, after having breathed out, there is normally a further 1000 cubic centimetres of air that can be forcibly exhaled!

THE NATURAL BREATHING PROCESS IS AS FOLLOWS:

By reducing the pressure exerted upon the lungs by the chest walls and using the muscles to increase the intrathoratic capacity of the lungs (chest capacity), a vacuum is created in the lung walls which allows air to enter. The volume of the thorax is also increased by the downward contraction of the muscles of the diaphragm (the base of the thorax).

Air enters through the nose and travels down the throat and the windpipe to the bronchial tubes. It is important to breathe through the nose – the mucous membranes lining the nose filter out a large proportion of dust and bacteria. Mucous also helps to fight off infection.

The air then moves into the lungs, where it enters millions of cells. Fresh oxygenated blood is absorbed into the bloodstream. The oxygenated blood then travels to the heart, which distributes it around the body, where it is absorbed by tissue and bone cells.

By increasing the pressure on the lungs by contracting the walls of the thorax (chest), the atmospheric pressure within the lungs is overcome and air is forced out of them. To control breathing, rather than consciously thinking of taking a breath, it is better to focus on the expansion and contraction of the walls of the chest and abdomen.

UNNATURAL BREATHING

Many of us have lost the art of healthy breathing. Tension, fatigue, unhappiness, fear and a frenetic lifestyle have contributed to making unhealthy breathing habitual. You may think that you are breathing correctly, but the chances are you are not.

Deep, slow, rhythmical breathing is central to the Yogic philosophy. In the Yogic system, the element that sustains life is known as "prana", which may be translated as "life force" or "absolute energy". This life force was also known to ancient schools in Greece, Egypt, Tibet and China.

According to the Yogis, the primary source of life force is found in the air; and yet it is not matter. Although found in its most free state in the air, it is not the air nor one of its chemical constituents. We are continually inhaling the air charged with "prana " and we are extracting it for our own uses. In ordinary breathing a modest amount of "prana" is extracted, but by controlled breathing it is possible to absorb greater amounts.

Yogis argue that not only is physical and mental strength increased, but that latent faculties can be developed and healing powers are enhanced: therefore, how we breathe has a more immediate and pronounced effect on our existence than any other physical function.

"Life is the breath. Therefore he who only half breathes, half lives." Yoga proverb.

THE ART OF HEALTHY BREATHING

Most of us breathe ineffectively. We do not derive the proper benefit from our breathing. This is partly because we do not know how to regulate our breath. When we breathe it is automatic, involuntary, unconscious; we must learn to breathe consciously, properly and rhythmically until it becomes part of our lives.

The Yogis, acknowledging the powerful effect breathing has on our bodies and minds, have developed various breathing techniques that fully utilize every part of the body and mind.

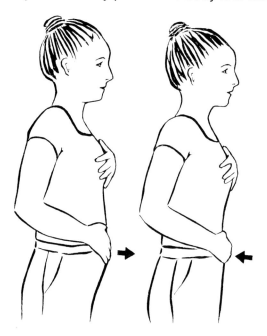

"The stomach moves out as we breathe in and moves back as we breathe out"

INHALATION

EXHALATION

Breathe in

Breathe out

DIAPHRAGM MOVES DOWN

DIAPHRAGM MOVES UP

A full natural breath fills the entire lungs, not just the upper part

POSTURE

POSTURE

For effective breathing, good posture is vital. Poor posture such as slumped shoulders, bent back or bowed head will impede the natural breathing process. If the body is mis-aligned, all the vital organs are affected, including the diaphragm. When we slump, the ribcage is unable to work efficiently, preventing the lungs from expanding fully.

As with dynamic art or athletism in its highest form, there is beauty in perfect posture. What nature gives us at birth we generally manage to lose as we become adult!

In some African countries, nat-ural correct posture as a child is continued into adulthood, as loads are very often carried on people's heads.

The idea that for "good" posture we need to look like a parade ground soldier is wrong. The act of forcing our shoulders back to supposedly stand straight not only looks unnatural but also inhibits breathing.

BREATHING AND THE ALEXANDER TECHNIQUE

When we become stressed we tighten our muscles. These might be any muscles, from the top of our head to our toes.

When we tighten the large sheaths of muscle that sur-round our ribcage, we squeeze the ribcage and prevent it from expanding and contract-ing freely as we breathe in and out. As we tighten and con-tract our muscles, we also constrict blood vessels, lymph vessels, nerves and the heart – all of which causes us to restrict the natural functioning and rhythms of the body.

All this pressure means that we are making it difficult to breathe and also to move. An Alexander Technique teacher will show you a relaxed way of standing, sitting, moving and attaining a good posture which will release tension and take pressure off the ribcage. Your breathing will then become easier and more natural.

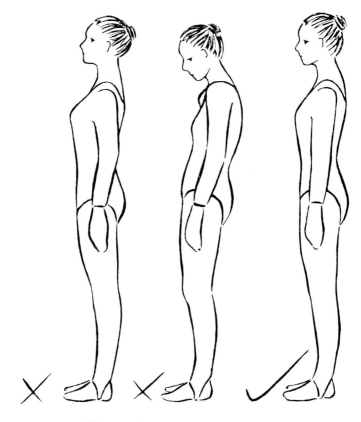

"For effective breathing, good posture is vital"

THE COMPLETE BREATH

"The difference between one deep breath
and many shallow ones is like the difference
between one loud cry of joy and many
sorrowful whimpers"

DE CHAK TSAO

THE COMPLETE BREATH

The Complete Breath is the fundamental breath of the Yoga science of breathing. The Complete Breath might sound an abnormal or forced thing, but it is quite the opposite – it goes back to the first principles – a return to nature.

The healthy adult tribesman and the healthy infant of civilization both breathe in this manner. It is the "civilized" man who has adopted unnatural methods of breathing. While the Complete Breath may feel unnatural at first, it will become part of our everyday life, occurring unconsciously and invigorating us throughout the day.

To perform a Complete Breath, sit or stand – aware of maintaining a good posture – and breathe in through the nostrils. To help fully experience the Complete Breath, it is useful to place your left hand on your stomach and your right hand on your chest. Inhale steadily, first filling the lower part of the lungs by lowering the diaphragm – feel your hand rise gently on your stomach pushing out (your right hand should remain still at this point). Then fill the middle part of your lungs, pushing out the ribs, the breast bone and the chest. Finally, fill the higher portion of the lungs.

With this movement the lower part of the abdomen will be slightly drawing in; this both supports the lungs and helps to fill the highest part of the lungs – notice your left hand gently sinking down.

It may seem that this part of the Complete Breath comprises three distinct movements. At first it may be easiest to consciously be aware of these three movements, but in time the movement will become

one, as inhalation becomes
continuous. It is important to
achieve a smooth action, avoiding any jerky movements.

The second stage of the
Complete Breath is to retain
the breath for a few seconds.
Then exhale quite slowly, drawing the abdomen in a little and
lifting it upwards slowly as the
air leaves the lungs. When the
exhalation is completed, relax
the chest and abdomen for a
few moments. With this
method of breathing, all parts
of the respiratory system are
brought into action, and all
part of the lungs are exercised.

It is not necessary to breathe
Complete Breaths with every
breathing cycle. In the early
stages, practicing Complete
Breaths just a few times a day
will benefit you when feeling
stressed. Indeed, the very act
of focusing on the Complete
Breath may be sufficient to
produce an immediate sense
of relaxation.

BREATHING EXERCISES

"A person who knows how to breathe is a person who knows how to build up endless vitality; breath builds up the lungs, strengthens the blood and revitalizes every organ in the body"

BUDDHIST TENET

BREATHING EXERCISES

The following exercises are based on long-established and recognised Yoga techniques. Yogis, probably more than any other group, have been involved in the investigation of the affects of various types of breathing – many of which effect our entire body in different ways.

The investigation has covered many centuries and the exercises that have evolved as a result are aimed not only at maintaining a good level of health and relieving stress, but also awakening and utilizing the vitality and energy that lies dormant within us.

THE CLEANSING BREATH

This exercise cleanses and ventilates the lungs, stimulates the cells and gives general health to the respiritory organs. It also refreshes the entire system.

This breath is used to complete most breathing exercises so it is a advisable to practice it well.

1. *Inhale a Complete Breath.*

2. *Hold the breath for a few seconds.*

3. *Position your lips as if you were about to whistle (do not blow out the cheeks). Exhale a little air powerfully through the opening. Pause for a moment and then repeat the process, continuing until all the air is exhaled.*

This breath can be refreshing and revitalising when you are feeling tired or run down. The full benefits come with practice, after which time you will be able to perform the breath naturally and easily.

THE ENERGISING BREATH

This breath stimulates the nervous system and develops vitality and energy. It sends an increasing nerve force to all parts of the body by stimulating parts of the body by stimulating important nerve centres.

1. *Stand upright.*

2. *Inhale a Complete Breath and hold it.*

3. *Hold your arms out in front of you with the muscles relaxed, applying just enough tension to keep them there.*

4. *Gradually pull the hands back towards the shoulders, contracting the muscles so that as the hands reach the shoulders the fists are clenched tightly.*

5. *With the muscles tense, extend the arms, pushing the fists out slowly. Then, keeping them tense, draw them back in rapidly. Repeat this several times.*

6. *Breathe out powerfully through the nostrils.*

7. *Do the Cleansing Breath.*

The power and effectiveness of this exercise is determined by the speed of the drawing back of the fists, the tension of the muscles and the full lungs. It is a wonderfully invigorating exercise.

THE RETAINED BREATH

This exercise, which involves holding the breath after the lungs have been filled with the Complete Breath can be very beneficial. It strengthens the respiratory organs but also benefits the nervous system and the blood.

Holding the breath occasionally replaces the air which has stayed in the lungs from previous inhalations. This helps to fully oxygenate the blood. Yogis recommend this exercise for cleansing of waste matter from the lungs, and for disorders of the blood, liver and stomach. It can also relieve bad breath.

1. *Stand upright.*

2. *Take a Complete Breath.*

3. *Hold the air for as long as is comfortable for you.*

4. *Exhale the air vigorously through the open mouth.*

5. *Do a Cleansing Breath.*

The length of time for which you can retain the breath will increase with practice. You may wish to time yourself to note the improvement.

NATURAL CHEST EXPANSION

If you bend over a desk or lean forward at work, it is quite usual for the chest muscles to become contracted. This can inhibit healthy breathing. The following exercise will help restore the natural shape of the chest and regain full chest expansion.

1. *Stand upright.*

2. *Take a Complete Breath.*

3. *Hold the breath.*

4. *Put both your arms out forward at shoulder height, clench both fists and hold them together.*

5. *Swing the arms out vigorously until they stand out in line with the shoulders and you are in the shape of a cross.*

6. *Bring the arms back to the front and then take them out to the side again. Repeat this four times.*

7. *Breathe out powerfully through the mouth.*

8. *Take a Cleansing Breath.*

Do not overuse this exercise.

THE WALKING BREATH

This is an invigorating exercise that can be practiced when you are walking. It is best not

41

practised when walking along streets full of traffic fumes.

1. *Walk at a steady pace with your head up, chin drawn in very slightly and your shoulders comfortably relaxed back.*

2. *As you walk, take in a Complete Breath over eight steps and count them mentally as you do so.*

3. *Breathe out over the next eight steps, again counting in your mind.*

4. *Do not follow on with the next Complete Breath immediately. Relax between breaths. As you continue walking, repeat the exercise. Carry on until you feel a little tired or you reach your destination. You can comfortably repeat this several times a day.*

5. *After having inhaled the Complete Breath you may wish to retain the breath for four steps and a count of four*

before breathing out. Use whichever method feels most comfortable for you.

MORNING EXERCISE

This is a simple, useful and stimulating exercise ideally practiced soon after waking.

1. *Stand upright and relaxed – shoulders back, head up, hands at your side.*

2. *Inhale a Complete Breath, and as you do so raise yourself up slowly and steadily onto your toes.*

3. *Hold your breath for about five seconds, retaining the position.*

4. *Slowly and steadily lower your heels to the ground while exhaling the air through your nostrils.*

5. *Take a Cleansing Breath.*

6. *Repeat five times.*

LUNG EXPANSION EXERCISES

A

1. *Stand upright with your arms by your sides.*

2. *Inhale a Complete Breath and hold it in.*

3. *Slowly raise your arms, keeping them straight until they meet over the head.*

4. *Hold the breath for about five seconds, keeping your hands above your head.*

5. *Slowly lower your hands to your sides, breathing out at the same time.*

6. *Take a Cleansing Breath.*

B

1. *Stand upright with your arms straight out in front of you.*

2. *Inhale a Complete Breath and hold it in.*

3. *Swing your arms back until they are straight out from your shoulders so that you are in the shape of a cross. Still holding the breath, swing the arms forward again. Repeat three times still holding the breath.*

4. *After the hands come together for the third time, breathe out vigorously.*

ALTERNATE NOSTRIL BREATHING

According to many ancient beliefs, this exercise is designed to:

- CLEAR THE NASAL PASSAGE AND SINUSES

- SOOTHE THE MIND AND EMOTIONS

- IMPROVE POWERS OF CONCENTRATION

1. *Sit comfortably and be aware of your posture.*

43

2. Exhale through both nostrils.

3. Place your right thumb over your right nostril and slowly breathe through the left nostril. Allow the breath to be deep and rhythmical, but do not strain.

4. Having inhaled, place your ring finger over the left nostril and pause briefly.

5. Release your thumb from your right nostril, breathing through it slowly and evenly.

6. Then pause briefly, and breathe through the right nostril.

7. Release the ring finger and breathe through the left nostril.

8. Repeat the exercise five times.

WHISPERED 'AH'

This exercise, by combining breathing techniques with gentle sound, is aiming to eliminate strain on the vocal chords. Without flexible breathing, you cannot have a flexible voice. The purpose of the whispered 'ah' is to free the jaw and allow the ribcage to expand. Regular practice will encourage the sound to bounce off the diaphragm.

1. *Place the tip of your tongue lightly between the lower teeth, allowing the main body of the tongue to rest on the roof of the mouth.*

2. *Slowly inhale, feeling your back widening, and your ribcage and diaphragm working. As you inhale, visualise a happy scene and try to smile.*

3. *Pause briefly, open your jaw, and allow a whispered 'ah' to flow out with the breath.*

4. *As you breathe out, try not to clench your jaw or tighten your throat. Imagine that the sound is floating through your body.*

5. *Repeat five times.*

You may choose to consult a Yoga teacher to develop and expand on these exercises, and techniques may differ a little. All these exercises are tried and tested, and are aimed at promoting health and well-being. If at any time you feel lightheaded or dizzy, stop immediately. If these symptoms continue, consult a doctor.

DO NOT ATTEMPT THESE EXERCISES IF YOU ARE HYPERVENTILATING. REFER BACK TO THE BREATHING TECHNIQUES IN THE SECTION ENTITLED "HYPERVENTILATION"

POWER BREATHING: MEDITATION

"If we are not breathing in harmony
with the our bodies, we are not living
in harmony with the world"

EASTERN PROVERB

POWER BREATHING: MEDITATION

WHAT IS MEDITATION?

For many people, the idea of meditation conjures up a passive or reflective act more akin to dreaming – it is in fact the very opposite!

This chapter has been called "Power Breathing" because meditation, when used in a correct and focused way, is a wonderful resource which enables us to counteract the effects of stress. Breathing in a controlled and focused manner in meditation is also an excellent way to enter the higher levels of consciousness.

With origins in the East, meditation is essentially heightened awareness. The practice has existed for thousands of years and was used originally within religions to achieve mystical consciousness.

Today, however, while still an important element in religions such as Buddhism and Hindiusm, and in contemplative prayer aspects of Christian religion, it is increasingly being turned to by individuals as a panacea for mental and physical health and to achieve a deep feeling of confidence and calm.

For many of us, with our minds constantly darting from one thought to another, the very idea of concentrating or focussing in order to relax the mind might at first seem a difficult task.

SO HOW CAN WE ACHIEVE MENTAL RELAXATION WHILE FOCUSING?

The act of focussing on breathing can lead to "Samadhi" – a mystical consciousness during which the meditator and the breathing become one.

Scientific analysis shows that focused awareness of breathing can calm and stabilise the nervous system. It can also provide mental clarity and a high degree of muscle relaxation. When focusing on the breath and allowing ourselves to turn inwards, we may be aware of thoughts and distractions. However, as we acknowledge them and recognise that they are not part of ourselves, we can let them pass us by.

LONG TERM BENEFITS OF MEDITATION:

- REDUCED ANXIETY
- GREATER EMOTIONAL STABILITY
- SUCCESSFULLY USED AS A THERAPY IN TREATMENT OF MIGRAINE, DISEASE AND DRUG ABUSE
- PROMOTES FEELINGS OF WELL-BEING AND CONFIDENCE

PHYSIOLOGICAL CHANGES DURING MEDITATION

- BLOOD PRESSURE NORMALISES
- HEART RATE DECREASES
- BLOOD LACTATE REDUCES (HIGH LEVELS OF LACTATE IN THE BLOOD INDICATE ANXIETY)
- SKIN CONDUCTIVITY DECREASES (SKIN CONDUCTIVITY IS AN AN INDICATOR USED TO ESTABLISH AN INDIVIDUAL'S DEGREE OF ANXIETY EG. AS IN LIE DETECTORS)
- THE BRAIN PRODUCES MORE ALPHA WAVES. THE KIND OF BRAIN WAVES WE EXPERIENCE IN PERIODS OF INTENSE MENTAL CLARITY, SOMETIMES EXPERIENCED JUST BEFORE SLEEP

THE ROLE OF BREATH IN MEDITATION

Previous chapters have shown how concentration on the breath can lead to a more relaxed and skilful way of handling day-to-day stress – both mental and physical. This can be taken a stage further by developing deep concentration on the breath, leading to the very highest states of meditation. In fact, a relaxed but alert state of mind is the foundation for success in meditation.

Meditational experience can be achieved in a number of different ways. Some groups advocate dance techniques, others might suggest focussing on a candle flame, while the practice of silently repeating a mantra (a word or phrase) is also successful.

A classic technique used by Buddhist meditation is called "anapanasati", literally meaning "mindfulness of the in-breath and the out-breath". The breath is an ideal object to use, as it is always there (so long as we are!). It is absolutely natural, and is usually unnoticed. One of the fundamentals of meditation is to raise awareness on a moment-to-moment basis.

In our daily life, such practice encourages a greater aware-ness of what is happening in the present – which in itself helps us to combat stress.

Breath is always moving, so the mind has to keep alert to follow it properly. Breathing can become infinitely subtle, encouraging the meditator's attention to grow finer and finer in order to be able to follow the breath completely.

MEDITATION: GETTING STARTED

There are few hard and fast rules for meditation. However, certain guidelines help.

1. Breathing is usually through the nostrils.

2. Eyes can be open or shut. If open, they should ideally be half open and focussed on a point comfortably in view.

3. Sit in a relaxed but upright posture, with the head tilted slightly forward. (If you choose to meditate while lying down, it is advisable to do so with eyes open, as closing them will probably make you feel sleepy).

WHERE TO MEDITATE?

Ideally choose somewhere where you can be alone and quiet and where you can remain without being disturbed.

WHEN SHOULD MEDITATION TAKE PLACE AND HOW LONG SHOULD IT LAST?

There is no "correct" period for meditation, many find two 20-minute sessions a day, one on the morning, and one in the evening ideal, but it is important not to feel rushed. If you can only manage a 10-minute session or, indeed, you feel sessions so rewarding that you wish to extend meditation to thirty minutes, then continue with that.

Whatever feels comfortable is usually beneficial. Do try to avoid meditation immediately after heavy meals, when some of the physiological energies of the body are involved with digestion.

MEDITATION POSTURE

Most Eastern meditators sit in the classic lotus position, but the majority of Westerners find this difficult, if not impossible to achieve. If you are not a student of Yoga (or have not had a circus career as a contortionist), it is best not to attempt this but to try one of the other positions illustrated

In most meditation postures it is important to attempt to keep the back straight. Apart from avoiding backache during long meditation, Yogis consider this allows "Kundalini", the latent spiritual energy in the body awakened during meditation, to rise through the body.

1. Sitting on a chair

Try to keep the back straight, without using the chair back as a rest, position your feet to help achieve the balance.

2. Lying posture

Lie flat on the floor, ideally on a carpet or rug and with your arms resting by the side slightly away from the body, preferably palms facing upwards. Allow your legs to move apart slightly, placing a book or rolled towel under your head allows a slightly flatter position of the spine.

3. Lotus position

You may find after a time that you wish to meditate while in a half lotus or lotus position. This is best practised under the guidance of a meditation or Yoga teacher.

HANDLING DISTRACTIONS

Most beginners starting meditation may be surprised how the mind flits around and will only remain focused on the breath for short periods. This is not because the mind is rebelling! It is simply because it is not yet used to focusing on a single simple subject. Practise will make this much easier.

While meditating, the way to deal with distracting thoughts or disturbances is to note and acknowledge each one as it appears and then to take your attention from it and gently refocus your attention on the breath.

This usually has to be repeated time and time again (and with some patience), until the mind can concentrate on the breath

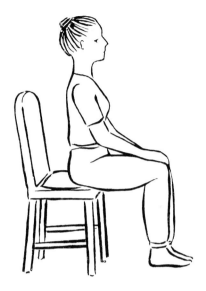

Sitting posture for meditation

Lying posture for meditation

for long periods, without wandering off. It is crucial not to take a rigid approach to distractions that inevitably occur during the breathing meditation practice, and try to stamp on them. This willl simply make them return all the stronger.

Allow disturbances to arise and disappear into the background, and concentrate on the breath which you have chosen as your "foreground". The process of noting distractions without tarrying with them will encourage them to subside naturally.

BALANCE

Meditation progresses when there is a balance of mindfulness (sometimes referred to as "awareness") and concentration. Whereas concentration is deliberately narrowed and beamed onto a single object, mindfulness has a broader function, lightly taking into account everything impinging on the senses at a given moment, including mental activities. It also means an awareness, for example, of where we are sitting and who is round about. Everything is accepted without judgement. Distractions and thoughts are acknowledged and allowed to go away freely.

Through this meditation technique, the mind eventually becomes very still and concentrated. When this is balanced by the right degree of mindfulness, the mind enters the different stages of deep meditation (or absorbtion) and insight – ending in complete freedom with "Nirvana".

Aways start, though, with gentle but determined concentration on the breath.

MEDITATING

Having settled into your meditational posture, gently bring your attention onto the breath.

There are various ways of doing this. Some schools ask students to place their attention on the breath as it flows in and out – at the tip of the nostrils. The attention is likened to a guard placed at the city gates, whose duty is to watch everyone who goes in and everyone who leaves.

Other schools don't focus attention on a single spot, but simply observe the whole breath as it goes in and out. Yet another variation is to anchor the mind on the breath by counting – either each breath, or the different stages the breath goes through on the way to the bottom of the lungs. Others repeat "in, in, in..." as it goes in and "out, out, out..." as it leaves.

These and similar approaches act as stepping stones towards the objective, which is to achieve a clear awareness of the sensations of the breath, and to keep the mind on it.

Three of the many different meditation techniques are described below. Choose one that suits you and try to stay with it for a while, rather than attempting different techniques every other day.

In these meditations, start by breathing slowly and rhythmically into the diaphragm; feel your tummy gently moving out with each exhalation. Your breathing rate will eventually decline and find its natural rhythm. Breathe through the nose and if distracted gently return your attention to your breathing.

A) BREATH COUNTING
B) FOLLOWING THE BREATH
C) BREATHING A MANTRA

A) BREATH COUNTING

In this method, complete sets of breath cycles are counted from one to 10, starting with "one" and continuing until you have completed 10 breaths.

The counting then continues restarting at one, and so on.

Counting should be silent and the count should be made with the inhalation or the exhalation (but consistently staying with whichever is chosen). If your mind wanders and you lose count, return to one and start again. You can either stay with this method or, after several weeks, move to the following technique.

B) FOLLOWING THE BREATH

Simply breathe, focusing attention on the way the breath enters and leaves the nostrils. Be aware of the different sensations with inhalation and exhalation, allowing your body to guide you to your own rhythm of breathing. Do not try to control it, just be mindful of it.

C) BREATHING A MANTRA

In this method, silently breathe a word using mantra "OM" (pronounced "OME" as in home). This is a Sanskrit word meaning universal spirit or consciousness and is said to be the primordial sound of the universe. During meditation think of the first part of the word "O" on the inhalation and the second part of the word "M" on the exhalation, simply continue doing this. "Hamsa", an alternative word, is said to represent the sound the breath makes on the inhalation "ha" and "sa" on the exhalation. The "m" joins up the two sounds, occurring naturally.

It may help choosing a word with which you are unfamiliar, or you may prefer a word that you know. A student experienced deep levels of meditation using as a mantra the word "bananas", although this is not recommended!

ENDING MEDITATION

When finishing a period of
meditation, do try to have a
short period of relaxation.
A few minutes is sufficient to
ensure that the benefits of the
meditation are not lost by
ending abruptly. Try sitting
with your eyes closed for a
minute or two – being aware
of nothing but your relaxed
body. Then continue with
your day.

There is no right or wrong
experience while meditating.
Just try to enjoy it, and do not
be impatient for benefits to
come; they will in time and
are well worth the effort!

CONCLUSION

CONCLUSION

The art of natural, healthy, relaxed breathing is one of the most powerful techniques that we have as a way of overcoming stress.

It is no surprise that for many cultures breathing has been so important over the centuries; but it is surprising how, in the so-called civilized world, our rush for an easy and comfortable life creates such stress, while we ignore one of the most fundamental and powerful life forces.

People who breathe healthily, look healthy; they are more relaxed and have a real sense of vitality. It is possible for any of us to improve our breathing, to do so creates a health-giving resource for life that costs nothing.

Life is simple – but we choose to make it so complicated.

By slowing down and creating a natural harmony within ourselves we can step away from the stresses in life. Even if this is only for a short period of time it can be beneficial.

We are all born with the ability to breathe in a relaxed and natural way. Its functioning has been developed and perfected over millions of years.

The tensions, frustrations, demands and speed of today's world takes a toll on all of us and for many people a healthy breathing pattern is one of the first things to suffer.

By returning to the basic healthy functions that nature intended us to use we not only find renewed health and inner harmony, we also have access to one of the most powerful stress-proofing skills in existence.

FURTHER INFORMATION

FURTHER INFORMATION

YOGA

Adult education centres throughout the UK are offering an increasing number of Yoga classes, at all levels. For further information contact your local education authority.

Iyengar Yoga

A method of Hatha Yoga (the practice of physical postures). For further information contact:

The Iyengar Yoga (Maida Vale) Centre
233A Randolph Avenue
London
W9 1NL
Tel: 0171 624 3080

Sivananda Yoga Vedenta Centre

The centre offers classes for beginners to advanced level in Asanas (postures), Pranayanas (breathing disciplines) and meditation. They also offer retreats and weekend workshops. Further details are available from:

The Sivananda Yoga Vedanta Centre
51 Felsham Road
Putney
London
SW15 1AZ
Tel: 0181 780 0160

TRANSCENDENTAL MEDITATION

Brought to this country in the 1950's by Maharishi Mahesh Yogi, transcendental meditation is a simple mental technique that allows deep rest for mind and body. It is best practiced for 20 minutes twice a day. For further information contact:

Transcendental Meditation
Freepost
London
SW1P 4YY
Tel: 0990 143 733

ALEXANDER TECHNIQUE
The Alexander Technique was founded around the beginning of the twentieth century by Tasmanian-born actor F M Alexander (1869–1955). When he encountered voice problems, he started out on what was to become a lifelong examination of how his mind and body worked together. The technique is now valued for its long-term effects – better health, natural healing and enhanced performance.

The technique focuses on the relationship between the head, neck and back. It releases tension by reconditioning mind and body responses, resulting in a well-balanced, free posture.

The Alexander Technique is good for stress-related illnesses, dealing with pain, breathing and voice problems as well as general health.

For further information contact:
The Society of Teachers of
Alexander Technique
10 London House
266 Fulham Road
London
SW10 9EL
Tel: 1071 351 0828

BUDDHISM

For details of Buddhist and Zen centres throughout the UK, contact:

The Buddhist Society
58 Eccleston Square
London
SW1V 1PH
Tel: 0171 834 5858

Recommended Bibliography

Benson, H, *The Relaxation Response*, Collins, 1976

Bohm, D, *Wholeness and the Implicate Order*, Ark Paperbacks, 1983

Easwaran, E, *Meditation – Commonsense Directions for an Uncommon Life*, Routledge and Kegan Paul, 1979

Hoare, S, *Yoga*, Macdonald, 1977

Humphrey, N, *Meditation, the Inner Way*, Aquarian Press, 1987

Iyengar, B K S, *Light on Yoga*, Harper Collins, 1966

LeShan, L, *How to Meditate, Thorsons*, 1983

Maslow, A H, *Towards a Psychology of Being*, Van Nostrand, Princeton, N J, 1962

Russell, P, *The Awakening Earth*, Routledge and Kegan Paul, 1982

Sole-Lewis, A, *Tranquillity and Insight*, Rider, 1986

Watts, A, *The Wisdom of Insecurity*, Rider, 1983

Whitaker, S, *The Good Retreat Guide*, Rider 1991 (frequently updated)

ALSO BY THE AUTHOR

Slim from within
Beat stress from within